ON THE MOVE...

DIESEL
TRUCKS

Written and photographed by Mark Rich

 CHILDRENS PRESS, CHICAGO

J629.2
R499d

Library of Congress Cataloging in Publication Data

Rich, Mark J
    Diesel trucks.

    (On the move)
    SUMMARY: Text and illustrations describe the
components of large diesel trucks and the skills
required to operate them.
    1. Truck tractors—Juvenile literature. [1. Trucks]
I. Title.
TL230.R5   629.22′4   78-7345
ISBN 0-516-03881-8

Photographs courtesy of International
Harvester: Front and back covers, pages
        7 (bottom), 10, 14, 20, 28, 32

Photographs courtesy of GMC: pages 13, 18

Have you ever wanted to drive a big diesel? Wow! Such size and power!

This is a brand new diesel, all clean and shiny. It is parked on a truck dealer's lot.

A new diesel tractor like this one will cost about $50,000! That's enough money to buy a big, new house!

A diesel "tractor" is the truck part of a truck-trailer combination. It is the part where the engine is and where the driver sits. The word "tractor" means the same thing as truck. What you've been calling "truck" all your life is really a tractor.

Diesel tractors are of two basic types. The first is the conventional body. The engine is placed in front of the driver's compartment.

The second type of tractor is called the cab-over. Most of the engine is under the driver's compartment. Cab-over trucks have flat fronts from the windshield all the way down the grille. Truckers call the cab-over tractor "snub-nose" or "flat-face."

Some trucks need more than one license plate because they travel in different states. Also, on many trucks you may see a lot of painted numbers. These are state and federal permit numbers that allow the truck to travel in different parts of the country.

cab-over

conventional

box trailer

Tractors pull three main types of
trailers. First is the standard enclosed
trailer, or what truck drivers call the
"box."

Second are tank bodies. These trailers
hold gasoline, milk, or some other liquid.

Flatbed trailers are the third type.
Flatbed trailers are flat with no sides or
tops. Cargo is set on them and lashed down
with heavy ropes, cables, or chains.
Drivers often call their trucks "rigs."
A "rig" can mean a tractor by itself or the
tractor and trailer together.

tank trailer

flatbed trailer

From the cab of a diesel you get a good view of the road. You can easily see over the tops of cars and pick-up trucks. That's good because tractor-trailers are harder to steer, stop, and get moving than smaller vehicles. The driver needs a good view of the road. He must know ahead of time what to expect and what to do.

The dashboard of a diesel tractor can be confusing if you are not a trained driver. There are many gauges. They tell you how the engine is working. There are a lot of light switches and many gears to shift.

There's a big difference between driving a passenger car and driving a diesel tractor!

Truckers that drive long distances cross-country sometimes want to sleep in their tractors. If they do, they can climb into a camper-like compartment in back of the cab. Truck drivers call a rig with a sleeping compartment a "Pajama Wagon!"

This diesel is a "Reefer." It is a refrigerated truck used for hauling things that will spoil if they are not kept cool. The refrigeration unit on this rig is the thin, black box with the grille that is attached to the front end of the trailer.

Many trailers have a wheel with a meter on it. The meter tells how far the trailer has been hauled.

Truckers must use these meters and their odometers (mileage indicators on the truck's dashboard) to keep careful track of how far they travel. They record where and when they stop. All this information is kept in a truck log book.

This is the back end of a diesel tractor. See how heavy the steel frame is? It has to be strong to hold the tons of weight it does when hauling a full load.

Look at all the springs attached to the axle. (The axle is what the wheels are attached to.) They are very heavy-duty thick steel, too!

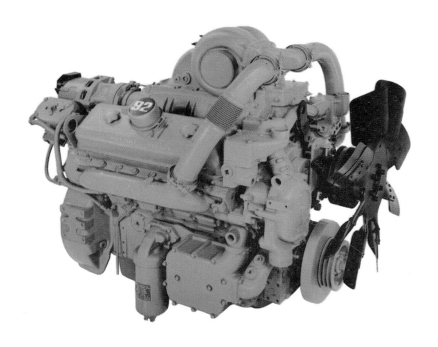

Diesel truck engines are very powerful. They range in horsepower from around 300 to over 500!

The hood of a diesel is sometimes the whole front end. Having the metal hood open out of the way makes it much easier to work on the engine.

19

From a car window a diesel rig seems really big. It is!

Here's a tractor-trailer with no load, speeding along the highway. A spare tire is chained to the trailer flatbed. If it weren't, it would bounce off onto the freeway. People driving along next to the truck wouldn't be too pleased with that!

Most trucks have wheel flaps. They keep rocks and mud from flying off the truck tires and hitting cars that are traveling nearby. Wheel flaps have saved a lot of car windshields from getting cracked!

Most trucks on the road now have CB's, or citizen's band radios. These are two-way radios that let people talk to each other while on the road.

With a CB, a driver can call for help if his truck breaks down or talk with other truck drivers who are in the same area. He can even find out from other CB'ers where the "county mounties" (county sheriffs) and state highway patrol cars are.

You can tell when a truck has a CB by the special antennas it has.

Here's a little CB truck talk:

Just south of Flagstaff, Arizona, this "low boy" (low trailer for hauling heavy machinery) has pulled off Interstate 10. This rig is "dead heading" (running without a load).

The driver is "kicking down" (shifting to lower gears) and will "lay on the air" (apply the brakes) when he comes to the stop sign.

Many trucks stop at a truck stop. Large truck stops located in big cities have places for the truck drivers to eat, rest, and get their trucks fueled, washed, and repaired.

See all the CB antennas on these diesel rigs?

The first tractor in this row has a clear plastic "bug guard" fastened just above its grille. This piece of hardware is designed to force air up higher over the cab so not as many bugs will hit the windshield.

Truckers must watch for special road signs. These two yellow signs say 14-0 and have arrows pointing up and down. These signs tell the driver that up ahead is a fourteen-foot bridge. If his truck is higher than fourteen feet, it won't get under! It would be very embarrassing for a good driver to get stuck, wouldn't it?

Truck drivers check maps and charts ahead of time. They know where there are low bridges. But just in case, these highway signs let them know.

Sometimes a truck is too high to fit under the bridge. Then the driver must pull off the highway and go around the bridge on a different road. Eventually he gets back onto the highway again.

The side fuel tanks, called "saddle tanks", on a diesel tractor hold fuel. Some of the larger tanks carry 150 gallons. If there is a tank on each side of the tractor, that totals 300 gallons. If that truck gets five miles per gallon of fuel, it has a range of 1,500 miles. It can go 1,500 miles before it has to stop and re-fuel.

Diesel tractors do not run on gasoline like most passenger cars. They run on diesel fuel, which is not as refined as gasoline. It is oilier and thicker than gas.

Diesel fuel is a little cheaper than gasoline. If gas costs 55¢ a gallon in Los Angeles, let's say, diesel fuel would cost about 49¢ there.

Big rigs don't get very good mileage. Some get as little as two or three miles per gallon of fuel. Even tractors getting the best mileage get only eight or nine miles to the gallon.

31

Big diesel rigs can haul a lot of weight. A
full load for a big tractor is 76,000 pounds,
or about the same weight as nineteen
pick-up trucks.

This diesel is cruising along the freeway, heading under a bridge. The top of the trailer is blackened on each side because of the exhaust from the engine's stacks.

When a truck gets really dirty, it needs a wash. There are special places to take care of dirty trucks like this one.

This is a truck wash. Under the roof, can you see the big, red-and-white, round brushes? As the truck is slowly pulled through the stall, these big brushes are turned on and pressed up against the tractor and trailer. They scrub it down with soapy water.

Then the truck is rinsed off, pulled out into the open, and men with big rags and ladders dry it off. Without ladders, they could only dry off the bottom half of the rigs!

Sometimes the front wheels are taken off two or three tractors, and they are hitched to another tractor. Then they can be moved together piggy-back style.

It is better if the trucks could haul loads back to wherever they are going—that way the company or people that own them could make some money. But it doesn't always work that way. Sometimes they have to be hauled back like this.

Flammable means easily set on fire. If a truck has "Flammable" on it, it is hauling gasoline, oil, kerosene, airplane fuel, or something that can burn easily or explode.

If a truck is hauling a flammable load, that word can easily be seen all over the truck and trailers. Flammable is a danger signal!

39

A diesel tractor has six to ten tires, depending on the type of load it is designed to haul. Tractors that pull only one medium-sized trailer will have six tires. Big rigs that tow one or two large trailers have ten tires.

This truck is a tandem, which is a tractor with two rear axles. See how the rear tires are mounted together in two's? Tires mounted together like that are called "duals."

The driver in this rig is starting to "pour on the coal" (step on the throttle) after making the turn.

41

If you want to be a truck driver, but don't know how to drive a truck, you can learn. This diesel rig is really a school on wheels! Expert drivers teach people how to shift gears, turn, back up, park, pull up to loading docks, and all the other things that truck drivers must know.

Maybe some day you'll be rolling along hauling heavy loads cross-country! If that's what you're after, good luck, and keep on truckin'!

GLOSSARY

Antenna: the device that receives and sends CB radio messages; also called an aerial.

Axle: the long metal rotating bar under the tractor, to which the wheels are attached.

"Box" trailer: a standard enclosed trailer, shaped like a box.

"Bug guard": a piece of plastic or other material fastened above a truck grille to force air over the cab and keep bugs from hitting the windshield.

Cab: the driver's compartment of a tractor.

Cab-over: a type of tractor with the engine under the driver's compartment; also called a "snub-nose" or "flat-face."

Cargo: the goods or items carried in the trailer part of a truck-trailer.

Citizen's band radios: two-way radios that broadcast on special frequencies, most commonly used by drivers.

Conventional body: a type of tractor with the engine in front of the driver's compartment.

"County mounties": CB slang for county sheriffs or law officers.

Dashboard: the panel in front of the driver, just under the windshield, with many gauges, switches, and knobs.

"Dead heading": CB slang for a truck that is running empty, without a load.

Diesel: short term for a tractor or truck that runs on diesel fuel rather than gasoline.

Diesel fuel: special fuel used in a diesel engine; it is thicker, oilier, less refined, and cheaper than gasoline.

Duals: tires mounted together in twos on a tandem tractor.

Engine: a machine that burns fuel to make a truck move.

Flammable: easily set on fire and likely to burn quickly and dangerously.

Flatbed trailer: a trailer, without sides or a top, on which the cargo is placed and lashed down.

"Flat-face": another name for a cab-over tractor.

Gauges: the instruments and dials on a dashboard that indicate how the engine and other systems are working.

Gears: the mechanisms used to control the speeds and directions (forward and reverse) of a vehicle.

Grille: a metal grate or screen that allows air to enter, but keeps out stones and other highway debris.

Hood: the metal covering over the engine, which is hinged so it can be opened and the engine worked on.

Horsepower: a unit indicating the size and power of an engine; one horsepower is equal roughly to the load a single horse can pull.

"Kicking down": CB slang for shifting down from a high-speed gear to a lower-speed gear.

"Lay on the air": CB slang for applying the brakes to slow down or stop.

License plate: a metal plate, issued by a state, carrying an identification number, and fastened on the front and back of vehicles.

Log book: a notebook drivers use to keep track of their trips—where and how far they have driven, where and how long they have stopped.

"Low boy": CB slang for a flat, low trailer used to carry heavy machinery.

Meter: an instrument on a trailer wheel that tells how far the trailer has traveled.

Mileage: the number of miles traveled by a vehicle on one gallon of fuel.

Odometer: a gauge on the dashboard that tells how many miles a vehicle has traveled.

"Pajama Wagon": a name drivers use for the sleeping compartment in a truck.

Permit numbers: identification numbers, issued by states and the federal government, that allow trucks to travel on state and federal highways.

Piggy back: several tractors hitched together, with the front wheels of all but the first tractor removed; in this way one driver (in the first tractor) can haul several tractors, saving time and expense.

"Pour on the coal": to increase speed, or step on the throttle.

"Reefer": a truck-trailer that is refrigerated to keep its cargo, such as foods, from spoiling.

"Rigs": what drivers sometimes call their trucks; it can mean the tractor alone or the tractor-trailer combined.

"Saddle tanks": fuel tanks fastened to the side of a tractor.

"Snub-nose": another name for a cab-over tractor.

Tandem truck: tandem means two; a tandem truck has two rear axles and thus four tires, two on each side.

Tank trailer: a tank-shaped trailer carrying a liquid cargo such as milk or gasoline.

Throttle: the pedal on the floor of the cab used to control the speed of a truck; sometimes called an accelerator.

Tractor: the front or truck part of a truck-trailer combination, containing the engine and driver's compartment.

Trailer: the back part of a truck-trailer, where the cargo is carried.

Truck: the front part of a truck-trailer; also called a tractor.

Truck stop: an area for drivers to park their trucks while they eat, sleep, or have their rigs worked on by mechanics.

Wheel flaps: loose, heavy pieces of material hanging behind the rear wheels of a truck; they keep mud, stones, and other objects from being thrown by the wheels onto vehicles traveling behind the truck.

INDEX

About The Author:

Mark Rich was born November 23, 1948 in Ray, Arizona, a small copper-mining company town. In 1952, the family moved to the Los Angeles, California area. He attended elementary and high school in the Los Angeles suburbs, and in 1966, began studies at Arizona State University in Tempe. He received a B.A. in Elementary Education from Arizona State in 1970 and an M.A. in Elementary Education from the same institution in 1972. He is currently finishing his 8th year of teaching in Phoenix, Arizona. He has taught 4th, 5th, and 6th grades.

His hobbies include traveling, writing, stereo, tennis, golf, and photography.